TABLE OF CONTENTS

1 MONDAY NIGHT MADNESS

With each win, the excitement grew. The Los Angeles Rams, behind third-year quarterback Jared Goff, were dominating their opponents. However, Patrick Mahomes, quarterback of the Kansas City Chiefs, also had his team on a roll. The teams began the 2018 season with matching 9–1 records.

On November 19, the Rams and Chiefs met in front of a national TV audience on *Monday Night Football*. And football

Jared Goff was a big part of the offensive explosion in the Rams-Chiefs game in 2018.

fans couldn't wait to see the two young quarterbacks duel.

"You can feel the hype and energy building," Rams receiver Robert Woods said prior to the game.

Playing at home, the Rams struck first as Goff hit Woods for a seven-yard touchdown. Later in the first quarter he connected with Josh Reynolds for another short touchdown pass. The Rams were up 13–0. But the action was just getting started.

Mahomes answered two minutes later with a 25-yard touchdown pass. The race was on. At halftime, the score was tied 23–23. Goff had thrown for two touchdowns. Mahomes had three.

Goff put the Rams back up early in the third quarter. He scrambled, then raced untouched

Goff celebrates one of his four touchdown passes on the night.

into the end zone for a seven-yard touchdown. But every time Goff put the Rams up, Mahomes and the Chiefs answered. Los Angeles took a 10-point lead into the fourth quarter, only to see Kansas City score 14 straight points. Another Goff touchdown pass put the Rams back up by three. Then with 2:47 left in the game,

The Rams and Chiefs were scheduled to meet in Mexico. However, bad field conditions there forced the game back to the Rams' home stadium, the iconic Los Angeles Memorial Coliseum. It has played host to two Olympics and two Super Bowls, including the first Super Bowl in 1967.

Mahomes answered. The Chiefs now led 51–47.

On this night, 2:47 proved to be plenty of time. The Rams got the ball at their 25. Over five plays, Goff led them to the Chiefs' 40. On the sixth play, he dropped back to pass. Wasting little time, he fired a long pass to Gerald Everett. The tight end caught it at the 15-yard line and ran into the end zone. Now the Rams led 54–51.

The Los Angeles defense closed it out from there. In one of the sport's all-time great shootouts, the Rams had prevailed. Only twice had a National Football League (NFL) game seen more scoring. And Kansas City became

Mahomes and Goff congratulate each other at the end of a historic night.

the first team to score 50 points in a game and lose.

Afterward, all anyone could talk about were the two young quarterbacks. They had combined to pass for nearly 900 yards. Goff threw four touchdown passes. Mahomes had six. However, Mahomes also threw three interceptions. A new era of high-flying offenses had taken over the NFL. Goff, it became clear, was leading the way.

AIRING IT OUT

Less than two minutes remained in the Monday night showdown between the Rams and the Chiefs. And Jared Goff's Rams trailed by three points. More than 77,000 fans at Los Angeles Memorial Coliseum watched as Goff took the snap from the Chiefs' 40-yard line. He shuffled back in the pocket. Then he set his feet and launched a long pass down the right sideline. The ball traveled 32 yards in the air, right into Gerald Everett's hands. The Rams tight end did the rest. He raced the final 15 yards into the end zone to give Los Angeles a 54–51 win.

2 GROWING UP GOFF

Jared Goff was born October 14, 1994, in San Rafael, California. He grew up nearby in a town called Novato. It's just north of San Francisco Bay.

Sports were always important to the Goff family. Jared's dad, Jerry Goff, was a professional baseball player. He even spent some time in the major leagues.

Jerry retired from baseball in 1997, and the family returned to the Bay Area in California. Both Jared and his older sister Lauren enjoyed sports.

Jared was a star quarterback at Marin Catholic High School.

Jared (16) played for the West All-Stars in the 2013 Semper Fidelis All-American Bowl.

Jared showed natural athletic talent from a young age. At Marin Catholic High School, he made the varsity team in three sports. Jared was a forward in basketball. He played shortstop in baseball. In football, Jared was quarterback.

Some thought Jared might follow his dad and play pro baseball. Instead, he proved to be even better in football. Jared became Marin's starting quarterback as a sophomore. In three years, he led his teams to a 39–4 record.

Jared was a leader on the field. He also showed a strong passing arm. Three colleges offered him scholarships. Jared decided to stay close to home.

He picked the University of California, also known as "Cal." It's the school where his dad played. And it was just across the bay in Berkeley.

STAYING COOL

As a kid, Jared was very competitive. However, he was known for keeping his cool. If he made a mistake, he didn't let it bring him down. And if he made a big play, he didn't celebrate too much. This helped him thrive in the high-pressure position of quarterback. In one game he led Marin to victory after trailing 17–0.

3 FROM GOLDEN BEAR TO RAM

Eager to get a head start on college, Goff arrived on campus in Berkeley in January 2013. When he got there, he joined a football team that wasn't very good. The Golden Bears had gone just 3-9 the season before. The school fired its longtime coach just weeks before Goff arrived.

This created challenges. It also created opportunities. During spring practice, Goff showed poise. Going against the older and more experienced players,

Goff stepped right in and started his first game as a freshman at Cal.

he was able to complete many of his passes. And in August of that year, he was named the Bears' starter.

Cal opened the season at home against No. 22 Northwestern. No true freshman quarterback had ever started his first game for Cal. And Goff had his moments in the game. His 39 completions that day would prove to be his career high at Cal. He passed for two touchdowns, too. However, he also threw three interceptions, and the Bears lost 44–30. Those themes continued throughout the season. Goff went on to set a handful of school passing records. But the Bears finished 1–11. It was their worst season ever.

The future was brighter, though. With Goff leading the way, Cal improved to 5–7 in 2014. The Bears had one of the best offenses in

Goff went out on top, leading Cal to a bowl victory in his final game.

school history. They were even better in 2015, finishing 8–5. Goff ended the season with another stellar passing performance in the Armed Forces Bowl. Cal beat Air Force 55–36.

By then, Goff's abilities were well known. He'd broken several team and conference

Goff and his family—sister Lauren and parents Nancy and Jerry—were all smiles after the Rams drafted him.

passing records. His statistics ranked among the best in the nation. That was even more impressive coming on a team without elite talent around him. Many scouts were eager to see Goff's strong passing arm in the NFL.

Goff decided he was ready to find out if he could cut it in the NFL.

The Los Angeles Rams traded for the top pick in the draft. They used it to select Goff. Like Cal, the Rams were not a very good team when Goff arrived. They were coming off nine straight losing seasons. The team was also in the process of moving to Los Angeles after 21 seasons in St. Louis. If any team needed a new franchise quarterback, it was the Rams. After serving as the backup for the first nine games, Goff got his opportunity.

GOFF OR WENTZ?

Leading up to the 2016 draft, many expected Goff and North Dakota State quarterback Carson Wentz to go 1–2. The question was who would be picked first. That ended up being Goff. The Philadelphia Eagles picked Wentz second. Wentz initially had more success. He started right away and made his first Pro Bowl in 2017. His team even won the Super Bowl that year, though Wentz missed the playoffs with an injury.

4 SUPER SEASONS

Goff started seven games in 2016. The Rams lost all of them. But struggles are common for rookie quarterbacks. Goff soon got a big break. After the season, the Rams hired a new head coach in Sean McVay. He was known for having a great offensive mind.

McVay determined that Goff had often been overwhelmed by a complex offense in 2016. The young quarterback also lacked confidence at times. So McVay designed an offense that was simple

The arrival of head coach Sean McVay helped speed Goff's development.

Goff made some big plays to help the Rams come back against the Saints.

yet effective. The Rams also added some talented players around Goff. As a result, Goff began having more success. This helped his confidence grow. Behind Goff and star running back Todd Gurley, the Rams had the league's highest-scoring offense.

McVay's impact showed in the standings, too. The Rams finished 11–5 in 2017. That earned the team its first playoff berth since 2004. Expectations for 2018 were even higher.

Goff and the Rams lived up to them early. They started the season with eight straight wins. Only the Kansas City Chiefs scored more points that season. But Goff memorably led the Rams past the Chiefs on *Monday Night Football*. With a final record of 13–3, the Rams looked like true contenders.

Behind their bruising running backs, they powered past the Dallas Cowboys in their playoff opener. That set up a showdown with the Saints in New Orleans. With a trip to the Super Bowl on the line, New Orleans jumped out to an early 13-point lead.

But Goff and the Rams battled back. Late in the fourth quarter, the Saints were driving. A controversial non-call for pass interference kept them out of the end zone. Instead the Saints kicked a field goal to go up 23–20.

With less than two minutes remaining, Goff got to work. He drove the Rams into field-goal range. Kicker Greg Zuerlein tied it. Then in overtime, the Rams drove into field-goal range again. This time Zuerlein's kick won it.

The win sent Los Angeles to Super Bowl LIII. Goff's promise as a franchise quarterback was already paying off. However, the Rams were no match for New England. The Patriots kept them out of the end zone in a 13–3 defeat.

In September 2019, the Rams offered Goff a new contract. It would keep him on the team for four more years, paying him $134 million.

The Patriots defense overwhelmed Goff and the Rams in the Super Bowl.

The 2019 season didn't go as well as the team hoped. Goff was inconsistent, and Gurley was injured. Still, the Rams managed their third winning season in a row. After many years of losing, Goff had the Rams back where they wanted to be.

TIMELINE

1. **San Rafael, California (October 14, 1994)**
   Jared Goff is born. He grows up nearby in Novato, California.

2. **Kentfield, California (2010–2012)**
   In three years as the starting quarterback for Marin Catholic High School, Goff leads the team to a combined 39-4 record.

3. **Berkeley, California (August 31, 2013)**
   Goff becomes the first Cal quarterback to start his first game as a true freshman. He goes on to start all 37 games the Bears play through 2015.

4. **Fort Worth, Texas (December 29, 2015)**
   In his final college game, Goff is named most valuable player as he leads the Bears to a 55-36 win over Air Force in the Armed Forces Bowl.

5. **Chicago, Illinois (April 28, 2016)**
   After trading up, the Los Angeles Rams select Goff first overall in the 2016 NFL Draft.

6. **Los Angeles, California (September 18, 2016)**
   Goff makes his NFL debut for the Rams, and he takes over as the team's starter a few weeks later on November 20, 2016.

7. **Atlanta, Georgia (February 3, 2019)**
   Goff and the Rams compete in the team's first Super Bowl since moving back to Los Angeles, but they fall 13-3 to the New England Patriots.

MAP

N

AT-A-GLANCE

Birth date: October 14, 1994

Birthplace:
San Rafael, California

Position: Quarterback

Throws: Right

Height: 6 feet 4 inches

Weight: 222 pounds

Current team: Los Angeles Rams (2016–)

Past teams: California Golden Bears (2013–15)

Major awards: Pro Bowl (2017, 2018), September 2018 NFC Offensive Player of the Month, Pac-12 All-Conference (2015)

Accurate through the 2019 NFL season and playoffs.

GLOSSARY

contract
An agreement between a team and player that determines how long the player is on the team and what he is paid.

draft
A system that allows teams to acquire new players coming into a league.

franchise quarterback
A quarterback capable of leading a team for a number of years.

rookie
A first-year player.

scholarship
Money awarded to a student to pay for education expenses.

scout
A person whose job is to look for talented young players.

scramble
To run around with the ball behind the line of scrimmage while looking for an open receiver.

varsity
The top team that represents a school in a given sport.

TO LEARN MORE

Books

Bankston, John. *Jared Goff*. Hallandale, FL: Mitchell Lane Publishers, 2018.

Bowker, Paul. *Best Super Bowl Quarterbacks*. Mankato, MN: 12-Story Library, 2019.

Meier, William. *Los Angeles Rams*. Minneapolis, MN: Abdo Publishing, 2020.

Websites

Cal Bears Football
www.calbears.com/sports/football

Jared Goff NFL Stats
www.pro-football-reference.com/players/G/GoffJa00.htm

Los Angeles Rams
www.therams.com

INDEX